FIFTY HATS
THAT
CHANGED
THE
WORLD

DESIGN MUSEUM

FIFTY
HATS
THAT
CHANGED
THE
WORLD

 **conran**
OCTOPUS

FIFTY HATS

FIFTY HATS

The hat has three main but not mutually exclusive functions. The first – and perhaps the most fundamental – is to protect against the elements and sometimes against a blow. A woolly winter hat and a bicycle helmet are in this respect allied. The second function is symbolic or emblematic – the crown and the chef's toque both indicate a role. The last – but not the least – function is aesthetic – for hats, perhaps like no other item of clothing, have the power to transform. All three kinds of hat are included in this book.

Sitting so prominently on the head and in such close proximity to the face, the hat can mesh with its wearer and his or her identity in an extraordinary way; each is accentuated by the other. It is this iconic vividness that perhaps gives the hat its prominence in our memories of events and personalities. Hats can act as a kind of frame for some very human moments in history.

It is perhaps this same vividness (together with the cult of informality, of course) that partly explains the decline of the fashion hat in the years after World World II. The hat attracts too much attention; it can say too much about the wearer. In more recent decades, however, millinery – the art of the *elegant* hat – has undergone a revival, led by some of the designers you will meet in this book, Philip Treacy and Stephen Jones among them. This is a renaissance that the Design Museum would like to celebrate here.

Hats can be variously practical, beautiful, whimsical … Here the British model Erin O'Connor sports British milliner Stephen Jones's jaunty Union Jack hat (2006) at the opening of the designer's exhibition 'Hats: An Anthology' at the Victoria and Albert Museum, London, in 2009.

MONOMAKH'S CAP

From the chef's high white toque to the cowboy's Stetson (see page 24), one of the primary functions of the hat is to connote status. This symbolic or emblematic role has its apogee in the crown: the usually precious headpiece that not only marks out kingship, but also in some cases, bestows it. Even without its wearer the crown retains the aura of power – hence its widespread use in graphic form as a symbol of the state.

Monomakh's Cap, which was the first crown worn to inaugurate Russian rulers and was used for four centuries, is one of the oldest surviving crowns in the world. Even in a country that rid itself of monarchy more than 90 years ago, it still retains its potent mystique. Crowns invariably attract myth, and according to one legend a Russian grand prince, Vladimir Monomakh, received the cap from a Byzantine emperor, Constantine IX Monomachus, who thus symbolically passed on the leadership of the Christian world. The workmanship is Central Asian, however, and the crown was much more likely the gift of Öz-beg, Khan of the Golden Horde.

The contrasting combination of rich filigree gold and the ring of sable fur is a fitting symbol of Russia, a sprawling country that straddles, two great continents both geographically and culturally.

Crowns are the ultimate status symbol in the form of a hat. Like the gold-and-sable Monomakh's Cap shown here, they were traditionally objects of elaborate material display, conveying the wealth, power and spiritual entitlement of the ruler who wore them.

HAT FOR MARIE ANTOINETTE

During the 1780s the milliner Rose Bertin (1747–1813) became one of the most influential women in France. Through her close relationship with, and influence over, her premier client, Marie Antoinette, she was able to manipulate the fashions of the day and expand her entrepreneurial empire. In so doing she incidentally established Paris as the centre of haute couture and set a template for the celebrity couturier that has, arguably, lasted to this day.

As a hat designer Bertin was hardly an innovator, but rather elaborated upon and literally enlarged the existing fashions of her time. In the Versailles of the late eighteenth century, it was impossible to say where a lady's coiffure ended and her hat began. Swags of velvet, satin and silk, festooned with jewels and rare feathers, sat atop, or rather meshed with, elaborate 'poufs' of padded and pomaded hair. Such towering, extravagant hairdos might be used to express one's patriotism, to commemorate celebrated events or simply to outstrip a rival at court.

Bertin's creations were scandalously expensive – many times a workman's monthly wages. It is not too much to say that, by encouraging the French queen's love of display and excess, this talented *marchande de modes* from the provinces helped to bring about the end of the monarchy.

One of Rose Bertin's elaborate headpieces for Marie Antoinette as shown in this detail from a painting by the Queen's portraitist, Elizabeth Vigée-Lebrun. Hairdo and hat fuse in an extravagant statement of fashion and femininity.

Much as Paris was, as the essayist Walter Benjamin famously wrote, the 'capital of the nineteenth century', the headgear of that century was the black top hat. At the hat's apogee in the 1860s and 1870s, metropolitan streets and other 'male' spaces such as the Stock Exchange were described as looking like forests of chimneys. The hat's assertive, thrusting and, yes, phallic shape formed a telling contrast with the archetypal female hat of the Victorian era – the protective, concealing bonnet (see page 22).

Early versions of the top hat first appeared in France and Britain in the late eighteenth century and were initially a dandyish fad. Extravagantly tall and coloured, their outlandish appearance caused an uproar whenever they were spotted in the street, leading to their French nickname, the *incroyable* ('unbelievable'). By the 1830s, however, the top hat had permeated throughout society and by the 1850s, under the patronage of Britain's eminently respectable and bourgeois Prince Albert, had thoroughly sobered into its now-classic black shape. By this time, too, silk – hatter's plush – had replaced the original beaver's or rabbit's felt.

Towards the end of the nineteenth century, the popularity of the top hat waned, replaced by more relaxed styles such as the bowler and the trilby (see pages 16 and 28). The top hat has had a vigorous afterlife, however – as formal attire at weddings and race days, and as livery for undertakers and doormen.

Right: By the early twentieth century the top hat – the classic headgear of the Victorian gentleman – was largely reserved for special occasions such as a day at the races. Below: One of the most famous top-hat wearers was the US President Abraham Lincoln, who used his to store letters and bills.

MᶜCLURE'S

For February.

ABRAHAM LINCOLN

Surveyor, Storekeeper, Postmaster and Legislator With 28 pictures, including

8 PORTRAITS OF LINCOLN

Stories by Robert Louis Stevenson Ian Maclaren Anthony Hope

The Autobiography of Elizabeth Stuart Phelps

Reminiscences of President Garfield By Mary Mitchell

And many other contributions and Pictures

10 Cents a Copy $1.00 a Year

FEZ

In the early nineteenth century the modernizing sultan of the Ottoman Empire, Mahmud II, decreed the abolition of the traditional male headgear, the turban, and its replacement by the tasselled red fez, which was already worn by some of his Greek subjects and by Ottoman sailors in North Africa. The decree met with widespread resistance, even from Western visitors to Constantinople, who missed the romantic exoticism of the turban and decried the 'ugliness' of the fez.

Through the nineteenth century, however, the Turks took to the fez with pride; despite its evident impracticality, it was even worn by soldiers in the Turkish army. Then, in 1925, the fez met a sudden reversal of fortune, as another Westernizing leader, the republican Mustafa Kemal Atatürk, suddenly donned a three-piece suit and Panama hat, and declared the fez illegal. Western hats of all kinds – from flat caps to panamas – flooded the Turkish capital as its inhabitants struggled to find something suitable with which to cover their heads while at prayer.

In the West the tasselled red fez has always had vaguely 'Oriental' connotations, from the Byzantine potentates depicted in Renaissance altarpieces to decadent artists lounging in opium dens. For some Muslims around the world, the fez – adopted when the Ottoman Empire was revered as the leader of the Islamic world – has remained a treasured symbol of identity.

Two men wearing the fez in a café in Djerba, Tunisia. North Africa is sometimes claimed as the original birthplace of this classic headgear.

BOWLER HAT (DERBY)

1848
Thomas and
William Bowler

What could be more English than the bowler hat, its unmistakable, rather clunky silhouette and unyielding form suggestive of all that is staid and stiff-upper-lipped? Its history and iconography, however, are altogether more complex and more fluid than that overriding image would suggest, crisscrossing class, cultural, national and even gender boundaries.

Even its origins in mid-Victorian Britain are mixed. The bowler was designed by London hatters Thomas and William Bowler for the famous London hat shop James Lock & Co. The hat had been commissioned from the shop by an English aristocrat, Edward Coke, for use by his gamekeepers, who needed a hard hat to protect them from overhead branches while riding. By the end of the century the bowler had migrated not only into the city, where it became the quintessential headgear of the plutocrat, but also to the American West, where, as the Derby, it was popular with settler and outlaw alike. Later, in the 1920s, the bowler wandered still farther, appropriated and assimilated by the peasant women of Bolivia and Peru, where it is now part of their traditional dress.

Meanwhile, closer to its original home, the somewhat pompous image of the bowler has inevitably drawn ridicule and subversion but also a kind of affection. From the tragicomic dignity of Charlie Chaplin's tramp to the Surrealist obsessions of the painter René Magritte, and from the androgynous allure of *Cabaret*'s Sally Bowles to the irony-laden apparel of *The Avengers*' John Steed, the bowler has flourished as a cultural icon even as it has vanished from everyday life.

Right: The bowler hat has undergone some surprising appropriations – here Aymara women wear the hat as part of their traditional costume while celebrating Bolivia's Independence Day.
Below: A more stereotypical wearer of the bowler hat.

BALACLAVA

Hats are not always about display; they can also be about concealment and disguise. The clichéd costume of a spy or secret agent includes a tilted broad-brimmed hat, and today celebrities vainly try to achieve anonymity by donning a nondescript baseball cap (see page 52). Taken to an extreme, the hat can became a kind of mask, blotting out the wearer's every feature except the eyes. The balaclava is the archetypal headgear in this respect.

The balaclava's original function was protective. Its origins lie in the woollen open-faced helmets shipped out to British soldiers fighting in the Crimean War (1853–6), where the biting cold caused almost as many casualties as the bullet. The hat – which took its name from a Crimean village and the site of a major battle – could easily be adapted to cover the mouth and nose, or even simply worn around the neck like a scarf. This adaptability continues to make the balaclava popular today among winter sports fanatics.

It is the eyeholes-only balaclava, however, that has become a modern icon. The balaclava-wearing, Kalashnikov-wielding terrorist is an unnerving and recurrent image on our TV screens – the epitome of our fears of an unknown, faceless aggressor who inflicts mayhem indiscriminately.

Subcommandant Marcos – the anonymous leader of the largely nonviolent Mexican revolutionary movement the Zapatista Army of National Liberation founded in 1994 – always conceals his identity beneath a balaclava. 'Marcos' has called his balaclava a 'black mirror' that reflects the multiple identities of the oppressed all over the world.

HARDEE HAT

Nineteenth-century military hats often showed a fastidious concern with decoration and insignia. They were, after all, primarily concerned not with protection, but with identity – quick-fire emblems that revealed in an instant the wearer's rank, role and affiliation. Who goes there?…

The Hardee is a case in point. First introduced as a hat for the US cavalry in 1855 and named for an influential army officer and tactician of the time, William J. Hardee, the hat became the official headgear of the entire US army in 1858. In the subsequent decade it was most closely associated with the Union side in the American Civil War (1861–5), although in practice it was widely worn by Confederate soldiers as well.

Its basic form was simple: a black broad-brimmed hat that was looped up on one side with an eagle and decorated with an ostrich feather on the other. Beyond that, however, the wearing of the hat was governed by a host of regulations. For one thing, the side on which the hat was looped depended on whether the wearer belonged to the cavalry, infantry or artillery – information that was confirmed by the colour of the tasselled cord. On the front of the cap was the branch insignia, such as the infantry's Jager (hunter's) horn. This was made out of brass for enlisted men or was embroidered to indicate an officer.

Unsurprisingly, out in the field such regulations were often relaxed or ignored. Some soldiers wore the Hardee *au naturel*, like a simple slouch hat, or abandoned it altogether for the cooler, more practical kepi.

John Wayne in John Ford's *Horse Soldiers* (1959) wears a regulation Hardee hat displaying the crossed sabres of the cavalry. The wearing of the Hardee was governed by an elaborate system of insignia and codes.

VICTORIAN BONNET

The bonnet is the classic headgear of nineteenth-century womanhood – the coy feminine counterpart of the masculine, go-getting top hat (see page 12). From the pioneering women of the American prairies to the genteel ladies of Elizabeth Gaskell's *Cranford* (1853), the bonnet was a head covering that served a purpose akin to the Muslim *hijab*, or headscarf. It ensured both modesty and privacy, while also providing a 'picturesque' frame for the face.

The bonnet was originally worn in the late eighteenth century as a domestic hair tidy but soon migrated out of the home as part of the simpler, pared-back fashions of the Napoleonic period. Wearing a bonnet in public, whether in church or to the shops, was *de rigueur* – a sign of purity among young marriageable women and of self-effacement among widows and spinsters. Some bonnet styles of the early nineteenth century – for example, the Parisian *invisible* or the British 'coal scuttle' – virtually sequestered women in public and prevented them from looking left or right without first turning their heads.

For all its association with modesty, the bonnet – with its gay-coloured ribbons and elaborate pleats and ruches – was also a much-desired fashion item. Many a young contemporary reader of Jane Austen's *Pride and Prejudice* (1813) would have secretly sympathized with the teenage tearaway Lydia Bennet and her hankerings after the latest bonnets from Paris.

For the Victorian woman the bonnet was a badge of modesty, in part because it concealed the hair – a conventional symbol of female sexuality. This photograph from around 1860 shows two older bonnet-wearing women; for widows and spinsters the bonnet also signified a sort of seclusion from the public gaze.

STETSON 'BOSS OF THE PLAINS' 1865

John Batterson Stetson

If ever there was a hat that could stand in for a whole culture, it is the Stetson – the broad-brimmed, high-crowned cowboy hat whose laconic, weather-beaten form evokes all the adventure, all the freedom and machismo, of the old American West.

Much of the Stetson's symbolic, not to say nostalgic, power must be put down to the circumstances of its birth, which were deeply rooted in the landscape itself. John Batterson Stetson (1830–1906) came up with the prototype while hunting in Colorado in the 1860s. Here was a hat that was made from a local material – beaver felt, originally – and perfectly adapted to the harsh environment, as it was lightweight, cool and watertight. Stetson put his idea into manufacture in Philadelphia in 1865, and the 'Boss of the Plains', as it was named, rapidly became a status symbol, treasured by cowboys as a badge of identity as much as for its practicality.

The original 'Boss of the Plains' was a rather plain affair – the brim flat, the crown low and smoothly rounded, and the band unadorned save for a discreet bow that showed which way around it should be worn. The cowboys who wore the hats, however, soon customized them to suit their own tastes, remoulding the brims or adding a deep 'Carlsbad' crease (high at the back and sloping towards the front) to the crown. Over time the Stetson company reflected such changes in the evolving design of the Boss itself, creating the iconic hat that would be mythologized in the Hollywood Westerns of the 1940s and 1950s.

Right: The hat that won the West. The Stetson still evokes the freedom and adventure of the cowboy's life out on the open plains. Below: In 1940s and 1950s Hollywood the cowboy hat was the emblematic headgear of American machismo, here represented by Gary Cooper.

CHEF'S TOQUE

In 1890 the French chef Auguste Escoffier (1846–1935) went to London to work as head chef at a luxurious new hotel on the Strand. This was the Savoy, recently opened by the impresario Richard D'Oyly Carte. During the Franco-Prussian War (1870–1) Escoffier had served as an army chef, and he now introduced, alongside his simplified interpretation of classical French cuisine, a military-style discipline to the British restaurant kitchen. The staff – from chef to *plongeur* – were organized according to the strictest hierarchy, and a clockwork order was imposed.

Part and parcel of this professionalization was Escoffier's insistence on a neat, spotless uniform, of which the chef's hat was the centrepiece. There is some debate about the exact origins of this extraordinary hat – the *toque blanche* as the pernickety might prefer to call it – but Escoffier's great forebear, Antoine Carême, seems to have been responsible for its wider adoption in France. The height of the hat related to the importance of the wearer in the kitchen 'brigade', and the number of pleats suggested the chef's skill – equalling the number of ways in which he could cook an egg.

The toque conveyed both discipline, and, thanks to its snowy whiteness, hygiene. But what it was mostly about was theatre – for the chef of the grand French tradition was, above all, a master of ceremonies, an arcane conjuror who could summon up, as if by magic, the spectacular dishes of haute cuisine. *Pêches Melba* or *fraises Sarah Bernhardt,* anyone?

Right: This painting by Sir William Orpen, RA, in 1921 – entitled Le Chef de l'Hôtel Chatham – shows the classic chef's uniform including a pleated toque, or chef's hat. Below: The rather simpler, chimney-like toque worn by many chefs today.

TRILBY

The soft felt trilby, with its deep-dented crown and flexible, undulating brim, is one of the enduring hats of the twentieth century. A close cousin of the fedora (which has a slightly wider brim) and the homburg (which has a curved brim), it has passed, in various guises and materials, through the generations and down the social classes – smart enough to wear with a suit, but with more than a whiff of informality.

The hat first became popular in the 1890s after appearing as a prop in George du Maurier's 1895 melodrama *Trilby* (based on his novel of the previous year), from whose title and heroine it took its name. The hat, like the show, was a sensation, its popularity – at least among the play-going classes – signalling the accelerating shift towards more relaxed styles of dress after the rigid codes of High Victorianism.

During the Edwardian period the trilby retained its somewhat bohemian glamour (it was popular, for example, among the artists and writers of London's Bloomsbury Group), and in the 1920s it became the favourite headgear of Britain's racing fraternity. Its democratization continued apace, and by the 1930s it was near-ubiquitous, famously worn, for example, by the dapper crooks of Graham Greene's *Brighton Rock* (1938). In the postwar era, after a period of eclipse, the trilby resurfaced in various youth subcultures of the 1960s.

Right: The British painter and war poet Isaac Rosenberg wearing a trilby in a self-portrait painted in 1914. At this stage the trilby was still very much a hat of bohemia, but after World War I it would spread throughout society. Below: Even today, whether worn by a man or woman, the trilby retains a certain jaunty casualness.

EDWARDIAN HAT

In Europe and the United States, the beginning of the twentieth century was, for the elite at least, a time of conspicuous consumption. This was nowhere more evident than in women's fashion, where swirling Art Nouveau dresses were balanced by full, towering headpieces that looked back nostalgically to the *ancien régime* and the extravagant creations of *modistes* such as Rose Bertin (see page 10).

At the centre of the millinery world, of course, stood Paris, where the fashion house Worth largely set the season's trends. Both London and New York, however, provided some competition, notably in the form of Lucile (Lady Duff Gordon, 1863–1935) and Anna Ben-Yusuf (c.1845–1909), respectively. While hat fashions, in fact, varied considerably during this period, the archetypal Edwardian hat was a gorgeous, amorphous mass of tulle, ribbons, flora and plumage, often raised on a 'pompadour frame' that was covered by waves of both natural and 'additional' hair. Large veils added to the frothiness of the whole ensemble.

It is easy to be critical of such confections – of their ostentation, of the restrictions they imposed on women's time and movement, and so on. But our nostalgia for the whole Edwardian look, evident in period films such as *A Room with a View* (1985), also helps to account for the enduring romantic appeal of the hats of this era.

The classic Edwardian hat, with its extravagant use of material and decoration, was an exercise both in aristocratic nostalgia and conspicuous consumption. It is perhaps no coincidence that in the age of the suffragettes millinery became backward-looking and restrictive.

AKUBRA

Alongside other 'Australiana' such as Drizabone dusters, boomerangs and Vegemite, the cork-strung Akubra is a key ingredient in the nation-continent's identity, and as such is considered by Australians with a mixture of affection and dismay. Famously worn by the movie folk hero Crocodile Dundee, the hat comes with such a heavy baggage of cliché that, today, it is well-nigh impossible to wear outside rural Australia without at least the pretence of irony.

Yet this high-quality rabbit-felt hat has a pedigree every bit as good as the American Stetson, to which it is closely related (not least because the Akubra company holds the licence to make the Stetson in Australia). It has its origins in the lightweight wide-brimmed slouch hats that were crucial to the livelihoods of nineteenth-century stockmen and swagmen, and thus is inextricably bound up with a key, sepia-tinged period in Australia's history – the pioneering days of nation-building.

The brand name Akubra was first used in 1912 by a Sydney-based company (originally based in Tasmania) that had been making versions of the hat since the 1870s. Throughout its history this family-run business has proved adept at exploiting the hat's mythic status, from celebrity-endorsement agreements such as that with the golfer Greg Norman (in 1986) to ongoing associations with international sporting events such as the Olympics.

Right and below: What could be more Australian than the Akubra? Stockmen wear the classic hat of the Outback.

TURBAN

With his taste for exotic and brilliant peacock-like colours, Paul Poiret (1879–1944) was the first great showman of haute couture, as well as an adept marketing man. He was also, however, a pioneer of dress reform, designing reinterpretations of the Empire gown that at last liberated women from the rigours of the Victorian corset and showed a new concern for wearability.

Poiret's repopularization of the woman's turban (another fashion staple of early nineteenth-century style) towards the end of the *belle époque* was showy and practical. In part, the vividly coloured turban played to the Orientalist fantasy that marked so much of the couturier's work as well as to the more general fashion for the exotic that erupted under the influence of the Ballets Russes. But the turban was also ideal daywear – especially when contrasted against the feathered-and-flowered 'piles' otherwise in favour at this time.

Certainly it is not too much to argue for Poiret's turban as a step towards the close-fitting cloche (see page 36), which in the 1920s would become the symbol of the liberated woman. It's only fitting, too, that the turban would later become the favourite headgear of that icon of Left Bank feminism, Simone de Beauvoir.

Poiret disseminated his designs by collaborating with popular illustrators such as George Barbier. Here the turban takes centre stage, helping to create the exotic, languorous look for which Poiret was famous.

LES MODES

Chez **POIRET**, par G. **BARBIER**

CLOCHE

Debate continues over whether the celebrated Parisian milliner Caroline Reboux (1837–1927) – then at the very end of her long career – was the first to introduce the cloche, but she undoubtedly helped to popularize it. By the early 1920s it had become an integral part of the 'flapper' look, alongside bobbed hair, bee-stung lips and a straight-cut chemise dress.

Bell-like hats were already in evidence before World War I, but through the 1920s they became increasingly minimalist, abandoning any hint of a brim – a style remote indeed from the extravagant confections of the Edwardian period. Pared back, practical and contemporary, the cloche chimed well with the boyish haircuts then in vogue, emphasizing the liberated androgyny of the New Woman as she began to experiment with what had previously been 'masculine' freedoms – sex, smoking and driving automobiles.

Haute couture versions of the cloche, of the kind that could have been bought in Caroline Reboux's shop in the avenue Matignon, were often made up of an intricate patchwork of felt, embellished perhaps by a discreet Art Deco diamond brooch. Worn snug against the head, low down across the eyes, the cloche emphasized the flapper's haughty, man-eating reputation by obliging her to hold her head high. Women were making an impression.

The helmet-like cloche hat helped to forge the strikingly modern flapper look of the 1920s.

VEILED CLOCHE FROM
SHANGHAI EXPRESS

Mr John (John P. John, 1902–93) was perhaps the greatest genius of cinematic millinery, able to evoke both character and mood, to provide focus and drama, as well as beguiling cinematographic texture.

Designed at the very beginning of his Hollywood career, this hat for Marlene Dietrich in Josef von Sternberg's stylish melodrama *Shanghai Express* (1932) was already a *tour de force*. When Dietrich's character, Shanghai Lily, first appears in a crowded Shanghai railway station, it is her remarkable veiled cloche that initially draws our attention. The sheath of feathers adds an inky blackness to the film's gorgeous chiaroscuro, while the hard helmet-like form and visor-like veil immediately suggest the independence and aloofness of the Dietrich character.

But that is not all. Once the film moves on to the train, the meanings of the hat evolve: the veil trembles in a corridor draught and close-ups reveal the flickering subtlety of the feathered cloche, just as Shanghai Lily's character itself softens and reveals its tremulous vulnerability.

Mr John would go on to create Hollywood hats over four more decades, most notably for Vivien Leigh in *Gone with the Wind* (1939), and in so doing generated an adoring clientele for his successful New York business, set up in 1948.

Marlene Dietrich as Shanghai Lily in the proto-film noir *Shanghai Express* (1932). The character's enigmatic personality was expressed through her clothes, and most especially her lustrous feathered cloche.

SHOE HAT

1937
Elsa Schiaparelli

The collaboration between the Italian artist-couturier Elsa Schiaparelli (1890–1973) and the Spanish Surrealist Salvador Dalí was one of the most creative and daring design partnerships of the twentieth century. Their joint ventures – which included the Lobster dress (1937) and the Lanterne handbag (1938) – married well with Schiaparelli's own eccentric oeuvre, which featured a whole string of surrealistic headpieces in the guise of inkwells, lamb chops and brimming baskets of flowers.

The 1930s was a golden age of experimental millinery, as designers indulged wholesale in a wilful plundering of historical styles and a playful approach to shape and form. In the midst of such anarchy, Schiaparelli and her creations kept their poise. The Shoe hat – another Dalí collaboration, and assuredly the most iconic of all Schiaparelli's hats – reproduced an upturned, oversized high-heeled shoe in felt to create a startling yet oddly elegant silhouette. As with all of Schiaparelli's designs, the Shoe hat was simultaneously a celebration and a send-up of the arbitrary, ephemeral nature of fashion design and its fetishistic neuroses.

In the renaissance of hat design that has taken place since the 1980s, it is perhaps Schiaparelli's bold, imaginative spirit that has proved the most influential over contemporary milliners rather than the more conservative, classical style of her arch rival, Coco Chanel.

The mistress of the sartorially surreal, Elsa Schiaparelli, sports her own creation, the topsy-turvy Shoe hat. Other wearers included Dalí's wife, Gala, and the editor in chief of the French *Harper's Bazaar* Daisy Fellowes.

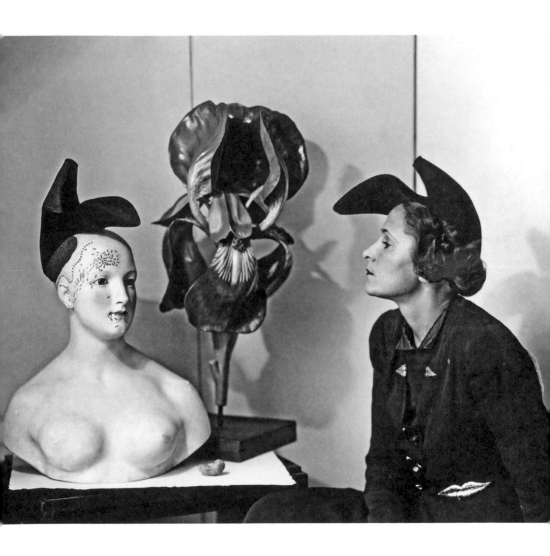

HAT FROM *THE WOMEN*

1939
Adrian Gilbert

From its very beginnings in the late nineteenth century, film has enjoyed a symbiotic relationship with fashion. 'We, the couturiers,' wrote the Parisian designer Lucien Lelong, 'can no longer live without the cinema any more than the cinema can live without us.' Movies exploited fashion to create glamour and spectacle, while fashion used cinema to generate consumer desire.

At no time was this relationship clearer than in the Hollywood cinema of the 1930s, especially in the work of the costume designer Adrian Adolph Greenberg (1903–59), widely known simply as Adrian or occasionally as Gilbert Adrian. His gowns, hats and shoes were given starring roles, and commercial copies were often released to coincide with the release of the film.

Adrian was particularly renowned for his work for Greta Garbo, whose grave blank beauty, he knew, was enhanced when framed by a hat. In *Romance* (1930) he created a gamut of ravishing if historically inaccurate designs to show her off. The film was a sensation, although perhaps less for the movie itself than for the neat velvet hat decorated with ostrich feathers that Garbo wore in one of the scenes.

It was for the 1939 George Cukor film *The Women*, however, that Adrian created his most iconic millinery designs. At various points the all-female cast sported an array of designs – from the classic to the outré – and in so doing provided a mirror for the aspirational clientele that was the bedrock of Adrian's ready-to-wear sales.

Rosalind Russell as the gossipy Sylvia Fowler in George Cukor's *The Women* (1939), wears one of Adrian's aspirational millinery creations. Adrian was just as able to make historical pastiches as he was to produce smart, bang-up-to-date designs.

TURBAN FOR CARMEN MIRANDA 1941

Lilly Daché

The classic Hollywood hat had to perform an extraordinary balancing act – it had to be striking, but not so much so that it stole the scene. The renowned movie milliner Mr John put the problem succinctly: 'A hat is the most dangerous thing in the world … A dress you can overcome. But you can't overcome a hat, because that's all you have, a face.' Hat and actress – or, more rarely, actor – had to work together.

The French-born Lilly Daché (1898–1989), who in Paris had trained with Caroline Reboux (see page 36) and in Hollywood often worked alongside the costume designer Travis Banton, was perfectly capable of making hats that complemented rather than upstaged an actress's face. With her series of flamboyant, fruit-and-feather turbans for the hip-swirling samba superstar Carmen Miranda, however, Daché seemed to throw all rules out of the window. Hallucinogenically surreal, these were hats, surely, with which no actress on earth could hope to compete.

But Miranda was able to do just that. In exuberant musical comedies such as *That Night in Rio* (1941) and *The Gang's All Here* (1943), the outrageous headdresses seem like nothing so much as extravagant outgrowths of the singer's personality – and as joyful and preposterous as the Samba Queen's famous voice.

Lilly Daché's tutti-frutti turban for Carmen Miranda in *That Night in Rio* (1941). This joyous eruption of fruit, glitter and glam embodies all the Latin extravagance of Miranda and the samba.

NEW LOOK HAT

1947
Christian Dior

After the devastation of World War II, Dior's New Look re-established Paris as the centre of the world's fashion industry and re-crystallized the myth of *la parisienne* as the very last word in chic. Although Christian Dior (1905–57) had only just brought out his first collection, and it had been heralded as 'such a New Look!' by *Harper's Bazaar* magazine, his opulent and sensual collections were in many ways far from 'new'. For all their sleek, sculptural modernity, the full, layered skirts, waspish waists and tight, crisp bodices looked back nostalgically to the ultra-feminine styles of the nineteenth and early twentieth centuries. They purveyed an elitist luxury that was remote indeed from the hard-pressed lives of most Parisian women at this time.

Accessories were crucial to the New Look style, and the hats, in particular, were strongly indebted to the past. Predominant in Dior's 1947 collections was a range of ivory-coloured low-crowned straw hats whose broad curved brims hung low across the wearer's face. The forms were simplified and abstract, certainly, but it is hard not to be reminded of the ribboned 'shepherdess' hats of the eighteenth century, so beloved of society painters such as Fragonard, or indeed of the traditional peasant women's hats worn in Indochina, France's Southeast Asian colony at the time.

In putting together the accessories for the New Look, Dior was strongly influenced by the tastes of his muse, the exotic, luxury-loving Mitza Bricard (1900–77), who from 1948 headed Dior's millinery department.

Rive Droite style. A *parisienne* models Dior's New Look on a cobbled embankment of the river Seine in Paris. Dior tempered the structural rigour of the New Look, hat and all, with a dose of gentle nostalgia.

COCKTAIL HAT

c. 1950
Svend for Jacques Fath

If the pillbox (see page 56) was the daywear hat of the 1950s, then its evening-wear counterpart was the cocktail hat – the small, elaborate and often veiled headpieces worn for parties and other formal occasions. But while the pared-back simplicity of the pillbox represented the confident, go-getting woman about town, the cocktail hat suggested that other icon of 1950s femininity: the exquisitely accessorized *femme fleur* ('flower woman') beloved of the post-war Parisian New Look designers.

This delicate hat, produced by Svend for Dior's arch rival, Jacques Fath (1912–54), is a lovely example of its species. Comprising a light wire frame woven with flowers of paper and cotton, and the merest suggestion of a maroon net veil, it was made at about the same time as the iconic Lily collection by Fath, whose full skirts were made to resemble flowers. The hat belonged to Lady Alexandra Howard-Johnston, the wife of the British naval attaché to Paris, who was regularly photographed on her husband's arm at state occasions and was invariably dressed by Fath.

'The only role a woman should have in fashion is wearing clothes,' Fath infamously wrote. With her perfect deportment and well-mannered beauty, the gloved and hatted *femme-fleur* was the ideal complement to the gilt-and-mirrored interiors through which she so effortlessly moved.

Svend's delicate flower-strewn cocktail hat for Jacques Fath was the perfect accessory for the idealized woman of the postwar period – ultra-feminine, passive and painstakingly elegant.

MARLON BRANDO'S BIKER'S CAP

In his turned-up Levi 501s, white T-shirt, leather jacket and pillowed cap, Marlon Brando, as bikers' gang leader Johnny Strabler, sent a shock wave across conservative America. Riding pillion on the media's sensationalized treatment of the 'outlaw biker' gangs – and in particular of the so-called Hollister Riot at a motorcycle rally in 1947 – the 1953 movie *The Wild One* presented audiences with a potent brew of rebellious youth, sexed-up masculinity and rough-and-ready, *déclassé* chic.

The cap, with its puffy camel-hair crown and leather visor, was a common bikers' style of the time, derived from working men's hats of the nineteenth and early twentieth centuries. Such bikers' caps had nothing to do with protection and everything to do with blue-collar machismo – the biker, after all, was the polar opposite of that other icon of the time, the super-suburbanite fedora-wearing 'Man in the Grey Flannel Suit'. The Brando look was a key moment, too, in the developing gay leather scene – itself an offshoot of the biker culture – although the jaunty hat was soon exchanged for the more fetishistic all-leather Muir cap.

An homage to Brando's cap was worn by the young motorcycling hero of the 2008 film *Indiana Jones and the Kingdom of the Crystal Skull*.

To modern eyes, Marlon Brando's biker's cap for *The Wild One* (1953) may seem curiously 'soft', even camp. At the time, however, it was the very last word in masculine sex appeal – oozing blue-collar oomph from the top of its camel-hair crown to the rim of its black leather visor. The motorcycle helped, too.

BASEBALL CAP

In the world of hats the baseball cap rules. Worn by all ages and both sexes, by sporting types and couch potatoes, by politicians and pop stars, by the ultra-fashionable and those with no fashion sense at all, the baseball cap has achieved a supremacy that can be matched only by those other ubiquitous pieces of Americana, the Big Mac and Coca-Cola.

The hat's very simplicity and practicality are the keys to its success, of course. This was a hat originally built for the sports field – it first reached its standard form in 1954, when it was officially adopted by Major League baseball – and as such it is lightweight, comfortable and cheap. The stiffened curved visor protects the wearer's eyes from the sun, while the adjustable strap allows for a good fit. What more do you want?

For its style*less*ness, however, the baseball cap has become the staple accessory of a plethora of urban street styles – from American hip-hop to the British chav. And enthusiasts such as Victoria Beckham are happy to be photographed wearing the cap… even if it is with a knowing irony.

The baseball cap is the most democratic of hats, migrating far from its origins on the baseball pitch (right) to become the ubiquitous headgear of the world and his wife, even when that wife is Mrs Beckham (below).

CHE GUEVARA'S BERET   1960

Guerrillero heroico, Alberto Korda's super-famous 1960 photograph of the Marxist revolutionary Che Guevara, has been called the 'quintessential postmodern icon'. Circulated, reproduced and appropriated seemingly ad infinitum across the globe, the image or its adaptations have appeared on everything from T-shirts to tea towels and the odd tattoo: a universal emblem of youthful idealism and glamorous rebellion. Its power lies in Che's face, of course – impassioned, Christ-like *and* sexy – but the black woollen beret also has its role to play. Austere and unembellished save for a tiny red star, and set rakishly askew on unkempt hair, the beret itself has become shorthand for Che and his spirit.

   The beret's association with left-wing politics predates Che: it was, after all, the vaguely louche headgear of Rive Gauche intellectuals such as Jean-Paul Sartre. It was never, however, the French national hat of the popular imagination. Its origins, while in France, lie at the country's utmost margins – among the foothills of the Pyrenees, where Basque peasants wore the *txapela* as protection against the constant mountain drizzle.

   Apart from Che, the beret is primarily associated today with the military. First adopted by the French mountain troops, the Chausseurs alpines, the beret has now become the ubiquitous headcovering of soldiers the world over – from the light-blue berets of the United Nations to the green version worn by the US Army Special Forces, better known as the Green Berets.

Perhaps one of the most iconic images ever made, Alberto Korda's photograph of Che Guevara associated the beret with revolutionary politics and heroic glamour for ever.

JACKIE KENNEDY PILLBOX HAT

1961
Halston

By 1961 the military-style pillbox hat had already featured in the collections of French couture houses such as Dior and Givenchy, but it was the pink wool example worn by Jackie Kennedy at her husband's presidential inauguration that was to establish it as the millinery must-have of that decade.

Ironically, Jackie Kennedy disliked hats, but protocol demanded that she wear one. Political expedience, too, insisted that it should be American – not French, as the Francophile First Lady would undoubtedly have preferred. For her inauguration-day dress and coat she turned to the well-established Oleg Cassini, but for her hat she chose the up-and-coming Roy Halston Frowick (1932–90), better known as Halston, who was then head milliner at the New York department store Bergdorf Goodman. Halston's hat designs were simple and minimalist, and the pillbox – which Jackie Kennedy wore, unusually, at the back of her head – was a perfect match for her neat geometric outfit.

Images of Jackie and her top-hatted husband walking through the January snow or being driven along the Washington boulevards appeared across the globe. Forget the President – the First Lady and what was quickly dubbed the 'Jackie Look' were a sensation. Halston, too, found his own career to be suddenly stratospheric.

The pillbox would remain the First Lady's signature hat throughout her husband's presidency. She was wearing yet another on an unseasonably hot November day in 1963, the day of his assassination in Dallas, Texas.

The presidential couple ride through Washington on the day of Kennedy's inauguration. The President went famously hat-less, but it was the First Lady's pink pillbox that really drew the world's gaze.

SPIRAL HAT

1961
Cristóbal Balenciaga

The craft of millinery has always concerned itself with geometry and volume, mathematical dimensions that are expressed artistically as sculptural or architectural form. At its most extreme, this can be seen in such bizarre creations as the *mazzocchio*, the wicker-framed Renaissance headdress whose perspectival complexities haunted the painter Paolo Uccello. In the twentieth century the Spaniard Cristóbal Balenciaga (1895–1972) was perhaps the designer who most clearly brought such concerns to the fore, in creations that combined consummate craftsmanship with an almost icy abstraction.

Balenciaga's analytical approach to design is exemplified by this spiral hat created towards the very end of his career. Taking the then-fashionable pillbox as its starting point, the hat is formed from a rising spiral of cool cream silk and is, in its kineticism and volumetric purity, a lucid translation of High Modernist principles. The simplicity of the hat, along with its eschewal of colour for line, belies the craftsmanship that underpins it – literally in the three internal hair combs that support its Tower of Babel-like form.

Balenciaga marries minimalism and millinery in this stark spiralling variation on the pillbox. Cool, crisp, even, this turns the hatter's craft into the art of abstraction.

KUFI CAP

Black is beautiful … From the mid-1960s the Black Power movement promoted pride in African-Americans' common heritage and their shared roots in the cultures of Africa. Racial pride encompassed appearance, too, and the adoption of 'Afro' hair and traditional African clothes, such as colourful dashiki robes and the kufi cap, became outward signs of a growing confidence, as well as – though not always – a political statement of black nationalism and of Pan-African identity.

The brimless round kufi is a traditional male headgear across much of West Africa and beyond, though it is worn especially by elders. The kufi is sometimes white, sometimes vibrantly patterned, and is sometimes made from the sacred cloth known as *kente*, woven by the Akan people of Ghana and the Ivory Coast. The cap has no particular religious affiliation, although it undoubtedly has spiritual associations, suggesting the wisdom and dignity of age.

In the United States the fiercer Pan-African connotations of the kufi have been tempered over time. The hat is now often worn at celebratory occasions such as weddings or graduations, or at more general African-American festivals such as Kwanzaa, another innovation of the Black Power movement.

Bangladeshi (right) and Moroccan (below) men wear the kufi hat. While the hat has strong associations with many Islamic cultures, the kufi is by no means exclusively worn by Muslims. In the United States, for instance, the hat is often worn as an emblem of African-American, indeed Pan-African, pride.

HAT FROM *MY FAIR LADY*

1964
Cecil Beaton and
Alice O'Reilly

In the post-war years, cinema and fashion continued to collaborate, though now as much off-screen as on-screen, in the mounting media obsession with the lives and looks of film stars like Grace Kelly. Perhaps the greatest fashion icon of the period, both on and off screen, was Audrey Hepburn, every one of whose films seemed to launch a trend – most famously the 'little black dress' of *Breakfast at Tiffany's* (1961).

Hepburn's flamboyant, outsized confection for the famous Ascot scene in *My Fair Lady* (1964) is surely the best-known hat in cinematic history. Designed by the photographer and set designer Cecil Beaton (1904–80), in collaboration with the Irish milliner Alice O'Reilly, the hat was a dazzling fantasia on the Edwardian picture hat – part parody and part celebration. Its dramatic black-and-white styling continued the monochrome theme of the whole Ascot set, which was inspired, Beaton said, by the 1910 'Black Ascot' races at which the entire elite wore mourning, following the recent death of Edward VII.

While the hat's whimsical nostalgia had little influence on developing trends in millinery, its emphasis on fashion-as-spectacle looked forwards, across several decades, to the extravagant catwalk creations of figures such as Jean Paul Gaultier and John Galliano.

Audrey Hepburn's clothes always played a key role in her films, providing a dazzling spectacle. Her supersized black-and-white hat for *My Fair Lady* was a surreal and nostalgic riff on an Edwardian theme.

COSMOS HAT

During the 1960s, as the space race between the US and USSR speeded up, the future was suddenly everywhere. From the Mathmos lava lamp (1963) in the living room to the bold, modular clothes on the catwalk, there was an all-out space invasion. Among the stars of space-age couture was Pierre Cardin (1922–), whose 1965 Cosmos collection was supposedly inspired by the first space walk by NASA astronaut Edward Higgins that same year.

The standout features of the Cosmos look included not only the much-copied sharply cut woollen tunic dress, but also a series of high-domed felt hats that paid tribute to what was fast becoming the icon of the decade, the spacesuit helmet. Some of the hats featured plastic visors, while still others took their cosmonautical model further, becoming thimble-like headpieces that covered the whole head, with just a shield-shaped panel cut out for the face.

For all that, Cardin's designs were as much about taking couture down into the streets as up into the heavens. The Cosmos hats and dresses were practical and fun, as well as aesthetically daring, representing a radical move towards simplicity and functionality in fashion, the long-term significance of which is only just being realized.

The space age lands on the catwalk. Pierre Cardin's helmets were a playful tribute to the astronaut's pressure helmet, with soft yielding felt replacing the hard polycarbonate shell.

PRINCE OF WALES'S INVESTITURE CORONET

The crowns of our imagination are high and stately things, so encrusted with jewels and pearls that the frame that carries them almost disappears. The coronet of Charles, Prince of Wales – made in 1969 by the gifted goldsmith (and former architect) Louis Osman (1914–96) – is by contrast a startlingly minimalist reinterpretation. Here the spiky 24-carat gold frame itself takes precedence, and the diamonds and emeralds are little more than sparkling points of light. Monarchy refracted through the prism of Modernism.

In reality, the coronet – futuristic as it first appears – carries the weight of tradition. The two half-arches (as opposed to the monarch's four) are ordained by convention, as are the cross-surmounted orb and the purple velvet and ermine 'Cap of Estate'. The jewels, too, are as symbol-laden as any medieval crown – the diamonds set around the orb reproduce the constellation Scorpio, the Prince's birth sign, while the diamonds set horizontally represent the seven deadly sins and the seven gifts of God.

The space-age feel of the design was apt – as the 20-year-old Prince was being crowned by his mother at Caernarfon Castle in Wales, across the Atlantic at the Kennedy Space Center on Merritt Island astronauts were making their final preparations for the first landing on the moon.

Prince Charles kneels before his mother wearing Louis Osman's modernist crown. The Queen, meanwhile, wears a Tudor-inspired headdress designed by the royal milliner Simone Mirman.

FLOPPY BERET

1971
Kenzo Takada

In the early 1970s, fashion jumped off its pedestal for a while and set about having fun. Designers celebrated extreme youth, pilfering the childhood wardrobe of pinafores and duffel coats, of woolly stockings and sou'wester hats, and taking delight in paintbox colours and geometric shapes. Against the background of the endless war in Vietnam and international terrorism fashion can perhaps be forgiven its bout of escapism, of burying its head, so to speak, in a metaphoric sartorial sandpit.

There is much more than a hint of the nursery in Kenzo Takada's outfits from 1971. The platform shoes, fun tights and fluffy primary-coloured coats suggested adults playing at being children, or perhaps the other way around. The icing on the cake was the oversized beret that made the wearer look as if she were trying on one of her mother's hats. Set off by a suitably giant-sized feather, this droopy, loopy hat was the perfect headgear for the wide-eyed ingénue about town.

Kenzo (1939–) was still at the start of his illustrious career, and he could afford a few carefree moments. If ever there were a hat to wear while splashing through puddles, this was it.

Millinery regression? Kenzo's whimsical oversized hats recall the headgear of the seven dwarfs in Disney's *Snow White* (1937). With their bright colours and soft, organic form, they certainly seem more suggestive of the children's nursery than the adult catwalk.

BELL BIKER

From the very earliest days of the bicycle in the late nineteenth century, cycling enthusiasts sought to protect themselves from head injuries by constructing rudimentary helmets. The earliest helmets, developed around 1900, were made out of soft criss-crossing leather straps that formed what was known as a 'hairnet'. This gave very little protection from an initial blow to the head, although at least it minimized grazes.

In the decades after World War II, the need for effective protective headgear grew more urgent as cyclists became ever more vulnerable on increasingly busy roads. In 1970 the Snell Memorial Foundation, a not-for-profit organization in the United States, laid down rigorous safety standards for cycling helmets. These were not achieved until 1975, when the US company Bell Sports created what effectively became the prototype for all modern cycling helmets. The Bell Biker used a foam liner made from expanded polystyrene (EPS) to provide effective shock absorption. This was encased in a rigid outer shell of the polycarbonate resin Lexan, which had earlier been used to construct the 'bubble helmets' used in the Apollo spacesuit helmet.

Rudimentary and unstylish as the Bell Biker may seem today, it was a revolutionary design. The subsequent development of the cycling helmet – be it teardrop aerodynamic styling or technical improvements such as ventilation, fit and stability – has been relatively superficial.

US company Bell Sports led the way in developing the first fit-for-purpose cycling helmet. Ubiquitous as it is today, back in the 1970s the cycle helmet seemed like a space-age curiosity.

QUEEN'S SILVER JUBILEE HAT   1977

Frederick Fox

Britain's Queen is perhaps an unlikely fashion icon, but for several decades her quiet but dogged patronage of some of Britain's and the Commonwealth's best hat and clothes designers has paid handsome dividends – not only for the designers individually and for British fashion generally, but also in the striking, dignified style she has managed to forge for herself. Pastels *can* be bold.

Hats have always been the leitmotif of the Queen's style, lending a measure of pomp and gravitas to even the most humdrum of occasions, as well as making her unmissable in a crowd – a key requirement. From Simone Mirman's Tudor-style headdress worn at Prince Charles's investiture as the Prince of Wales in 1969 (see page 66) to Philip Somerville's purple chevalier-style hat for the opening of the new Scottish Parliament building in 2004, her hats – and they have always been unmistakably *hers* – have rarely struck a false or dull note.

The Australian Frederick Fox (1931–) was, until his retirement in 2002, another of the Queen's mainstay milliners. In 1977 he provided the hat for the first major anniversary of the Queen's accession – the Silver Jubilee. In essence a soft pink cap with the addition of a cluster of green-stemmed tulips flowing down to the neck, it has an almost Schiaparellian playfulness that is restrained only by the sheer beauty of the craftsmanship.

In 1977 Frederick Fox's pastel-pink tulip hat for the Queen's Silver Jubilee caused a sensation, though not entirely a positive one. From today's perspective, however, it appears as an exquisite piece of millinery, finding a nice balance between majestic display and demure simplicity.

PORK PIE HAT

The chirpy, streetwise pork pie hat is closely related to those other two man-about-town hats: the fedora and the trilby (see page 28). Its distinctiveness lies, of course, in its 'pork pie' shape, featuring a flattened top with an indent running all the way around and a stiff turned-up brim.

Originally introduced in the nineteenth century, the pork pie hat is best known for its venerable associations with the music scene. Its earliest connections in this respect are with jazz and blues, and the hipster cool of figures such as the saxophonist Lester Young, for whom Charles Mingus wrote the elegy 'Goodbye Pork Pie Hat' (1959). Then, in the 1960s, the hat became an attribute of the 'rude boy' dancehall scene of downtown Kingston, Jamaica, alongside sharp suits and narrow ties. From the Caribbean the style migrated to London, where the pork pie established itself as a staple of the ska, mod and skinhead scenes.

In 1977 the UK band the Specials led a ska revival and donned the classic ska uniform of mohair suit, loafers and, of course, the classic pork pie hat. The hat's retro charm has intermittently made it a popular street-style statement ever since.

Jerry Dammers, founder and keyboard player of the Specials, sports a pork pie hat at a gig in the late 1970s. The pork pie hat was a key ingredient in the whole ska look.

PIRATE'S BICORNE

1981
Vivienne Westwood
and Malcolm McLaren

From the very beginning, hats have loomed large in the rich and eclectic oeuvre of Vivienne Westwood (1941–). Their top billing arises partly from her curiosity about, and meticulous research into, historical dress, for which hats can so often stand in as a sort of shorthand. But there is also Westwood's childlike love of theatricality and masquerade – looking at her work, it is hard not to imagine the designer up in a metaphoric attic, rifling through a dressing-up box and trying on every prop she can find.

It is not surprising, then, to find the dashing bicorne – the two-cornered hat worn by admirals and pirates alike – as the figurehead of her first own-name collection. By the late 1970s Vivienne Westwood had moved away from the anarchic, pornographic energies of punk to forge the softer, more approachable style of New Romanticism. In 1981, in the company of her long-time collaborator, Malcolm McLaren (1946–2010), she produced the scene's definitive style statement – the Pirate collection – the vibrant prints, billowing drapes and edgy, androgynous glamour of which swept like a high-seas gale across the stately prow of the fashion industry.

Westwood's pirate's hat takes us straight into the gleeful world of pantomime, of course. But it also suggests something more subversive. By donning the admiral's hat, the pirates of old were aping the establishment and appropriating a symbol of power for themselves. Much the same could be said of Westwood and her haute couture.

'Ahoy there, me hearties!' Westwood's pirate look – and the bicorne hat – caught the postmodern spirit of masquerade that dominated the 1980s. Dressing up and playing with identity were the name of the game on the clubbing scene.

MESH FLOPPY HAT

1987
Maria Blaisse
for Issey Miyake

The relationship between hat and wearer is often static. Once placed squarely on the forehead, pulled down firmly towards the eyes or stealthily secured with hatpins, the hat, to a large degree, stays put. The influential Dutch designer Maria Blaisse (1944–) creates headpieces that explore a more dynamic relationship between object and body. Hers are hats that can be moulded by the wearer or that move as the wearer moves, occupying the fluid, nebulous space between self and not-self described by the British fashion historian Elizabeth Wilson. For her work Blaisse typically uses surprising, even unappealing materials – such as rubber and foam – but manages to draw out a hidden kineticism and beauty.

In 1987 the Japanese designer Issey Miyake invited Blaisse to create hats for his 1988 spring/summer shows in Tokyo and Paris, for which the signature piece was a ghostly unbleached-linen dress. Part of Blaisse's response was a lightweight floppy-brimmed hat made out of piña, or pineapple fibre – a material that has a long history of use as a textile, most notably in the Philippines. From this gauzy material, Blaisse conjured up a hat whose fragile, mobile beauty not only perfectly complemented Miyake's collection, but also suggested new possibilities for the hat as a responsive, interactive garment.

Maria Blaise's beautiful mesh hat for Issey Miyake was a piece of kinetic art; its shimmering, diaphanous form flowed and transformed as the wearer moved.

HAT FOR DIANA, PRINCESS OF WALES

1987
Philip Somerville

For three decades the New Zealand-born milliner Philip Somerville (1930–) has been one of the stalwarts of the world's hat-making industry. His bold, unfussy hats occupy the classical middle ground of the European millinery tradition, with a clientele ranging from the crowned heads of Europe to celebrities such as Jerry Hall and Joan Collins. Since 1995 he has been the holder of a royal warrant as milliner to the British Queen.

Somerville's formative relationship, however, was with Diana, Princess of Wales, for whom he began to design hats on a regular basis after opening a salon in London's Bond Street in 1987. In the autumn of that year Diana wore one of his creations during a state visit to Berlin. Its striking double crown and bold contrasting colours marked a decisive move away from the more demure creations the Princess had hitherto worn, indicating how Diana was beginning to assert her personality in a way that she had not previously essayed. It was in short a kind of sartorial declaration of independence that foreshadowed things to come.

From our perspective the hat may seem somewhat tarnished by associations with the blousy, overemphatic styling of the 1980s. At the time, however, its clean geometry and bracing colour were like a breath of fresh air.

Black and primrose yellow may seem a surprising colour combination, but this striking hat was a sign of the more forthright and determined persona that the previously demure Princess was beginning to adopt in the late 1980s.

HARRIS TWEED CROWN

1987
Stephen Jones for
Vivienne Westwood

Vivienne Westwood's Harris tweed autumn/winter show of 1987 provided not only one of the watersheds of her career, but also one of the most memorable catwalk spectacles in fashion history. Its subversive deployment of that most venerable of British textiles, Harris tweed; its introduction of the Westwood staple, the corset; and its use of celebrity models such as Patsy Kensit and Sara Stockbridge whipped up the audience into a state of near hysteria.

The star design of the show, however, was not by Westwood herself, but by Stephen Jones (1957–), at that point already an established milliner (see page 88) whose clientele included none other than the darling of the age, Diana, Princess of Wales. In this light, Jones's Harris tweed crown may seem especially cheeky. In reality, however, its playfulness was celebratory rather than derogatory. With its bright, cartoonish colours, squishy woollen form and fake ermine trim, it had very little in common with the savage take on 'God Save the Queen' released a decade earlier by the Sex Pistols, the punk band managed by Westwood's partner, Malcolm McLaren.

Both Jones and Westwood specialize in a peculiarly British response to Britishness – at once subversive and traditionalist, both ironic and affectionate – and the tweed crown offers a neat summation of their spirit.

Westwood model and muse Sara Stockbridge sports Stephen Jones's gorgeously subversive tweed crown, as photographed by the influential British fashion photographer Nick Knight. Their collaboration provided one of the iconic images of the 1980s.

ROYAL ASCOT HAT

1989
David Shilling

Ladies' Day at the Royal Ascot horse races is one of the great events of the British calendar and a showcase for all that is glamorous, spectacular and perhaps cartoonish in millinery. For many years no Ladies' Day was complete unless Gertrude Shilling (1910–99) – nicknamed the 'Ascot Mascot' – appeared in the Royal Enclosure in one of her son's fabulous, show-stopping hats.

David Shilling (1956–) began to design Ascot hats for his mother when he was just 12. His inspiration was the oversized black-and-white hat worn by Audrey Hepburn for the Ascot scene in *My Fair Lady* (see page 62). In subsequent years the hats grew ever more outlandish and surreal, variously featuring a dartboard, a cheeseboard and, here, a whole picnic hamper complete with strawberries and champagne flutes. The hats were paired with equally extravagant dresses – the hamper, for instance, topped off one made from Astroturf.

Gertrude's Shilling's headline-grabbing entrées were not always the best advertisement for her son's more conventional designs, sold through his London boutique and US department stores. Over several decades however, mother and son were determined to add a splash of glamour, fun and downright camp to what otherwise might have been a conventional society affair.

The 'picnic hamper' hat worn by Gertrude Schilling for Royal Ascot's Ladies Day in 1989. David Schilling's creations for his mother continued the venerable tradition of the Surrealist hat inaugurated by Elsa Schiaparelli in the 1930s (see page 40).

BEANIE

The archetypal headgear of grunge, the early 1990s music movement, the beanie was the antidote to every fashion hat ever made. After the excess and flash of the 1980s, this unisex, back-to-basics oversized skullcap became the countercultural crown of Generation X – the epitome of the thrift-store ethic.

Grunge clothing, like the grunge music it complemented, was about being laid-back, about getting on with the stuff that really mattered, rather than worrying too much about making a splash. The beanie was just something to wear on your head, although perhaps (you might have secretly suspected) it also served to cover up greasy, unwashed hair. After all, 'Kurt Cobain was just too lazy to shampoo,' as the music journalist Charles R. Cross once quipped.

Of course, every non-statement has the habit of soon becoming a statement, and over the years even the unassuming beanie has become a staple of fashion cool. Still youthful, still lazy, yes, but a *fashion* accessory nonetheless.

From grunge to high fashion – a DKNY model wears a beanie on the catwalk in 2008.

'WASH 'N' GO' HAT

By the late 1970s hats had been toppled from their pedestal on the international fashion scene. Much of the credit for their renaissance during the following decade can be given to the British milliner Stephen Jones (1957–), whose alternately flamboyant, poetic and anarchic creations once again put hats centre stage – on the catwalk, on the magazine cover and on the heads of the icons of the age. Whether they are theatrical pieces for pop legends such as Boy George, show-stopping *jeux d'esprit* for the likes of John Galliano or elegant yet quirky pieces for high-profile clients such as Diana, Princess of Wales, in Jones's hands hats have regained their age-old cultural vibrancy.

The 'Wash 'n' Go' hat represents a quieter but nonetheless potent moment in Jones's wide-ranging oeuvre – typical of the whimsical lyricism he is able to instil in his designs. As ever, he shows his readiness to experiment with unconventional, surprising materials: here using clear acrylic to create the effect of a splash of water across the wearer's head. The hat plays, of course, on the primary function of headgear – protection – but turns it surrealistically on its head. As Jones himself would be the first to admit, hats are nothing until they are worn, but in that meeting of inanimate and animate a magical act of metamorphosis can occur.

Poetry in motion. Stephen Jones's clear acrylic 'Wash 'n' Go' hat reproduces the effect of a freeze-framed splash of water. The result is at once curious and beautiful.

WIDE-BRIMMED SOMBRERO FROM *FOUR WEDDINGS AND A FUNERAL*

1994
Lindy Hemming

Andie MacDowell could not fail to win Hugh Grant's heart in this wide-brimmed hat worn for 1994's British romantic comedy hit *Four Weddings and a Funeral*. Boldly scaled yet formally understated, this midnight-black summer sombrero compensated, some would claim, for the underwhelming performance of the actress who wore it.

During the late twentieth century, hats gradually dwindled from everyday use as well as from the cinema. It is therefore only apt that they should make such a dramatic re-entrance in a film centring on the two occasions, weddings and funerals, where hats have continued to be worn. Wedding hats, especially, are accessories where otherwise-conservative dressers feel that they can 'splash out' on something extraordinary, even joyous. The funeral hat, by contrast – more demure, often veiled and usually black – continues the tradition of covering the head in church.

The costume design for *Four Weddings* was by Lindy Hemming, who would go on to win the Academy Award for best costume design for another English movie, Mike Leigh's *Topsy-Turvy*, in 1999.

The model and actress Andie MacDowell was the epitome of early 1990s style. Her black big-brimmed hat for *Four Weddings and a Funeral* caused a flurry of imitations and for a time was seen at weddings up and down Britain almost as often as Auden's 'Funeral Blues' (another of the film's iconic moments) was read at funerals.

FEATHERED HAT FOR ISABELLA BLOW

1996
Philip Treacy

The Irish milliner Philip Treacy (1967–) is evangelical about hats: 'Everyone has a head so everyone has a possibility to wear a hat and you feel good in a hat. People feel better for wearing them.' Treacy may be renowned as the creator of all that is glamorous and avant-garde, but he also produces ready-to-wear pieces that are sold in high-street chains. Everyone has the right to be glamorous once in a while.

Nonetheless, it is perhaps for his more spectacular creations that Treacy will be remembered and most especially for his work with his patron and friend, Isabella Blow, the influential English magazine editor. For Blow he designed a series of startling, even surreal headpieces that might be said to have revived the grandiose traditions of eighteenth-century court millinery (see page 10). One even took the form of a fully rigged sailing ship, the outlandish size of which prevented her – in true Versailles style – from getting through doorways.

This black feathered hat represents a slightly less grandiloquent moment in Treacy's work for his friend. Yet the razor sharpness of the feathers and the almost mathematical precision of the plume as it sweeps across Blow's face and upwards like a wave make for a vivid, declamatory statement for all that, drawing our attention, but then deflecting any lingering gaze. Treacy is rarely quiet. Well-crafted drama is the key to his art.

Right: Isabella Blow once claimed that she liked wearing Treacy's hats because they prevented strangers from getting too close to her. This dramatic feathered hat certainly gives the impression of acting as a kind of barrier between the wearer and the world. Below: This disc hat from 2001 provides another typical Treacy statement: formalist, dramatic, and elegantly crafted.

TWEED FLAT CAP

For much of its history of 400-odd years, the wedge-shaped woollen flat cap was the near-universal headgear of the British working classes. Even today its popular association is with the pigeon-fancying, whippet-racing northern British male – a stereotype that stubbornly endures. For all that, in reality the flat cap has all but vanished as working-class gear. For some time it clung on only as country casual wear, donned by the 'gentry' to go with the padded Barbour jacket and green Hunter Wellington boots. In this respect Prince Charles is the iconic flat-cap wearer.

In recent years, however, the flat cap has moved out of its country retreat and stormed the city as a trendy urban fashion statement. It appeared first, worn back to front, as an element of hip-hop style, and in the 2000s it was showcased – especially in its tweedy avatar – by such celebrities as Madonna and David Beckham. Its revival *might* have something to do with a nostalgia for country living or even a resurgence of conservatism. Perhaps. But the primary reason is the hat's strong, flattering profile, which looks good on both men and women – from whatever class they come.

Right: For a time the tireless pop chameleon Madonna adopted the British gentry look, together with the tweed flat cap, as part of her love affair with the country and one of its more famous sons, Guy Ritchie. Below: Traditionally the flat cap has transcended class, worn on the country estate as well as out on the football terraces.

HAIRTS/ICONIC HEADS

2003
House of Flora
with Neil Moodie

Through the twentieth century there was surprisingly little collaboration between milliners and hairdressers, and the two disciplines have sometimes seemed divided by mutual incomprehension. This has not always been the case. Back in the eighteenth century, for example, *modistes* such as Rose Bertin (see page 10) worked alongside hairdressers to create headpieces that integrated hat and hair in an extravagant, seamless whole.

In 2003 a collaboration between Flora McLean (1971–), founder of the avant-garde millinery studio House of Flora, and editorial hairstylist Neil Moodie sought to reintegrate their divergent disciplines. The duo first met while working on a photographic shoot for *Face* magazine and soon after embarked on an ongoing series of pieces (initially named 'Hairts' but later renamed 'Iconic Heads') that fused their creative specialisms.

Each of the hats re-creates a famous hairdo – whether the Marcel wave from the 1920s, Farrah Fawcett's fabulous 1970s flick or Elvis Presley's rockabilly quiff. McLean is well known for her playful use of experimental materials such as latex and PVC (vinyl), and the Iconic Heads show the same inventiveness, using wood veneer to suggest the rigid curls of Fawcett's flick, for example, or sequins to create the Brylcreem gloss of the Presley quiff. We are all postmodernists now, and the Iconic Heads let us plunder the hairdos of the past and try them out – even if just for a day.

Hats and hairdos collide in Flora McLean and Neil Moodie's Iconic Heads. The Marcel (right) – a homage to the classic 1920s hairdo – was first seen in 'Millinery in Motion', part of the exhibition 'Hats: An Anthology by Stephen Jones', and won McLean the Jerwood Contemporary Makers prize in 2010. Below: The Rykiel pays tribute to the redhead French fashion designer Sonia Rykiel.

LED HELMET

2007
Hussein Chalayan

The catwalk hat can be much more than a flourish in the unfolding spectacle and drama of a fashion show. It can explore the possibilities of headgear itself, displaying technical or aesthetic innovation in its own right or breaking new conceptual ground. The LED helmet from the 2007 autumn/winter collection of Hussein Chalayan (1970–) was just such an offering.

Chalayan's catwalk shows are known as much for their poetry and intellectual rigour as for their beautifully crafted, adventurous clothes and technical ingenuity. This collection was no exception, offering a meditation on the often fraught relationship between a clothed, protected body and a global environment under pressure. The Plexiglas helmet suggests both human vulnerability and ingenuity in the face of environmental change. An internal ring of LED lights illuminates the whole transparent hemisphere to reveal a frosty print of delicate flowers, so that light and decoration provide a bubble of summertime, even in the depths of climatic gloom.

This helmet is a piece that asks us to rethink what the hat is for and how its age-old role of protection might be extended.

What can hats be and do? Through the technology of LED lighting and the ingenuity of design, Chalayan's hemispherical helmet brings the ambience of summer even to the harshest of winters.

MULTICOLOURED POMPOM HAT 2007

Søren Bach

In 2008 the cult Icelandic singer Björk appeared on stage at London's Hammersmith Apollo wearing an oversized headdress of rainbow-coloured pompoms that looked like nothing so much as a cloud of balloons in the sky. Björk is known, of course, for her patronage of the avant-garde, but here she had surpassed herself. This was a hat that teetered on the brink of absurdity, but which by some sleight of hand created an atmosphere both carnivalesque and poetic – like something out of a children's picture book.

It is in the evocation of the intense and dreamlike that the hat's creator, the Danish hairdresser-turned-milliner Søren Bach, excels. A 2007 graduate of London's Royal College of Art, Bach has made something of a speciality of working with fur – a luxury material with a long pedigree in hat making – and using experimental dyeing techniques that he has helped to develop. The result is a series of dramatic, transformational pieces that work on the fringes of craft, art and performance.

Recently, Bach has turned to the world of folklore and fairy tale. These are darker creations – both literally and metaphorically – exploring a world of decadent eroticism and strange metamorphoses that could be straight out of the pages of Angela Carter.

Playful, beautiful, absurd … Søren Bach's cloud of rainbow-coloured pompoms added just the right note of lyrical, blissful surrealism to Björk's magical, experimental music making.

HELMET HEADPIECE

2008
Franc Fernandez for
Brian Lichtenberg

Predicting fashion trends can be a futile business, and certainly the most shocking or the most eye-catching pieces do not always – or even often – indicate the shape of things to come. For this reason it would be foolhardy to point to the angular, geometric headpieces created by the young Los Angeles-based designers Franc Fernandez and Brian Lichtenberg as harbingers of the future of hat design. Perhaps the most that one can say is that these exciting, unisex designs encapsulate a certain notion of the zeitgeist and explore new possibilities of what a hat is.

Despite his youth Lichtenberg is already a well-established fashion designer, known for slick body-conscious clothes that are snapped up by celebrities such as M. I. A. and Lady Gaga. Fernandez, by contrast, has worked primarily as a graphic designer. He started making hats for his own forays out onto LA's avant-garde club scene. In 2008 Lichtenberg invited Fernandez to collaborate with him in the creation of hats for an upcoming fashion show, the aesthetic of which he described as being a hybrid between 'motocross and lingerie'.

The helmet headpiece is like a computer-generated 3D model, a graphic interplay of line and shape. At one level it plays on the protective function of a hat, but does so only to subvert it and create something that looks unsafe both to wear and to be around. Like Lichtenberg's edgy, brittle clothes, the headpiece offers an ambivalent image, simultaneously suggesting spiky aggression and fragile vulnerability – a potent symbol of the post-9/11 condition.

Franc Fernandez and Brian Lichtenberg's geometric headpiece is a postmodern tribute to the American football helmet. Functionality is stripped away to reveal the bare bones of the form – sexy, aggressive and so, so American.

HAT FOR ARETHA FRANKLIN

2009
Luke Song

Usually it is the First Lady who draws all the sartorial attention at a US president's inauguration (see page 56). In 2009, however, Michelle Obama – for all her elegance and fashion sense – was upstaged by the 66-year-old singer Aretha Franklin and her grey woollen hat with its outsized rhinestone-studded bow. As big and bold as Franklin's personality, it was the perfect headgear for a televisual age. Even before the Queen of Soul had finished belting out the patriotic hymn 'My Country, 'Tis of Thee', both the hat and its designer, the South Korean-born American milliner Luke Song (1972–), had made an instant worldwide mark. In the following days and months, orders for the hat came flooding in, although Song refused to make any duplicates, only a cheaper version in satin and horsehair, and with a slightly smaller bow.

In essence this great splash of a hat is what African-Americans know as a 'crown' – a showy headpiece worn to church as a mark of pious respect. And the 2009 inauguration *was* as good as a religious occasion, as millions across the United States and indeed the world greeted the advent of the first African-American US president with a near-messianic surge of optimism and hope. This in part explains the success of Song's dove-grey big-bowed hat – a way of bringing just a little bit of that hope closer to home.

Aretha Franklin and her grey bowed hat take centre stage at President Obama's inauguration in 2009. The hat was every bit as bold and as vigorous as her mighty-lunged delivery of 'My Country, 'Tis of Thee'.

RIBBONED CITYSCAPE HAT

2010
Noel Stewart

'People often draw parallels with sculpture and fashion,' the British milliner Noel Stewart (1978–) has said, 'but, in the case of millinery, it's a genuine love match.' With this hat, however, Stewart's explicit analogy is with architecture – and indeed with a whole urban landscape. The acetate crown comprises a huddle of skyscraper silhouettes from which a deep fringe of videotape ribbons flutters earthwards like ticker tape at a nocturnal carnival. This is a hat both dramatic and disconcerting, blurring the boundaries between fashion, art and architecture, then throwing in cinematic references for good measure.

Stewart is among the most daring and innovative milliners working today – not entirely surprising given his pedigree, which includes periods working for the British designer Dai Rees and for Stephen Jones (see page 88). Stewart launched his own collection in 2003. In his subsequent work he has contrasted sublimely surreal *coups de théâtre* such as the ribbon cityscape hat with quieter but no less inventive pieces that combine traditional forms with unusual materials and eye-catching twists.

Stewart's unusually eclectic range of inspiration encompasses everything from Surrealist art and Hollywood films to Modernist architecture and Mesoamerican headdresses. And the result? Hats that are often challenging and even baffling, but never less than exhilarating.

Noel Stewart assembles a bricolage of references for this theatrical headpiece, ranging from a Mayan headdress to the skyscraper skyline of Fritz Lang's *Metropolis* (1927).

INDEX

PICTURE CREDITS

The publisher would like to thank the following contributors for their kind permission to reproduce the following photographs:

2 williamselden.com; 7 Samir Hussein/Getty Images; 9 akg-images; 11 Chateau de Versailles, France/Giraudon/The Bridgeman Art Library; 12 Private Collection/Barbara Singer/The Bridgeman Art Library; 13 Underwood & Underwood/Corbis; 15 Roger Wood/Corbis; 16 Ted Spiegel/Corbis; 17 George Steinmetz/Corbis; 19 Paul Fusco/Magnum Photos; 21 Silver Screen Collection/Getty Images; 23 Royal Photographic Society/Getty Images; 24 Hulton Archive/Getty Images; 25 Frank Lukasseck/Corbis; 26 Handout/Getty Images; 27 ©Royal Academy of Arts, London/ph:John Hammond; 28 Rex Features; 29 Courtesy of Sotheby's Picture Library; 31 Hulton Archive/Getty Images; 32 & 33 Bill Bachman/Alamy; 37 Hulton-Deutsch Collection/Corbis; 39 Paramount/The Kobal Collection; 41 ph:Andre Caillet/Fundacio Gala-Salvador Dali; 43 MGM/The Kobal Collection; 45 20thC Fox/Everett/Rex Features; 47 Willy Maywald/Keystone, France/Gamma/Camera Press, London; 49 V&A Images/Victoria and Albert Museum, London; 51 Columbia/The Kobal Collection; 52 Sipa Press/Rex Features; 53 Bettmann/Corbis; 55 ph:Alberto Korda ©ADAGP, Banque d'Images, Paris & DACS, London 2010; 57 Leonard McCombe/Time Life Pictures/Getty Images; 59 V&A Images/Victoria and Albert Museum, London; 60 Stefan Auth/imagebroker/Alamy; 61 Andrew Holbrooke/Corbis; 63 Warner Bros/The Kobal Collection; 65 Express Newspapers/Getty Images; 67 Adam Woolfitt/Corbis; 69 Kenzo; 71 Bell Sports; 72 Nils Jorgensen/Rex Features; 73 Rex Features; 75 NBCU Photobank/Rex Features; 77 Robyn Beeche; 79 Issey Miyake courtesy of Maria Blaisse; 81 Tim Graham/Getty Images; 83 NK Images; 85 Allsport UK/Getty Images; 87 Chris Moore/Catwalking; 89 justinephotography.com; 91 Polygram/Channel 4/Working Title/The Kobal Collection; 92 Cavan Pawson/Evening Standard/Rex Features; 93 Miguel Reveriego/trunkarchive.com; 94 Bert Hardy/Picture Post/Getty Images; 95 Humberto Carreno/Rex Features; 96 williamselden.com; 97 ph:Derek John; 99 Chris Moore/Catwalking; 101 Yui Mok/ Press Association Images; 103 ph:Hedi Slimane for Vogue Hommes courtesy of Brian Lichtenberg; 105 Ron Edmonds/AP/Press Association Images; 107 Noel Stewart

Every effort has been made to trace the copyright holders and we apologize in advance for any unintentional errors or omissions, and would be pleased to insert the appropriate acknowledgment in any subsequent publication.

CREDITS

First published in 2011
by Conran Octopus Ltd
in association with
The Design Museum

Conran Octopus Ltd
a part of Octopus Publishing
Group, Endeavour House,
189 Shaftesbury Avenue,
London WC2H 8JY
www.octopusbooks.co.uk

An Hachette UK Company
www.hachette.co.uk

Distributed in the United
States and Canada by
Hachette Book Group USA,
237 Park Avenue, New York,
NY 10017 USA

British Library Cataloguing-
in-Publication Data.
A catalogue record for
this book is available
from the British Library.

Text written by:
Robert Anderson

Publisher:
Lorraine Dickey
Consultant Editor:
Deyan Sudjic
Managing Editor:
Sybella Marlow
Copy Editor:
Alison Wormleighton

Art Director:
Jonathan Christie
Design:
Untitled
Picture Researcher:
Anne-Marie Hoines

Production:
Caroline Alberti

ISBN: 978 1 84091 569 3
Printed in China